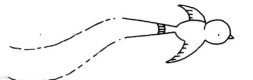

Practical Pre-School

Planning for Learning through Summer

Rachel Sparks Linfield and Penny Coltman
Illustrated by Cathy Hughes

Contents

Published by Step Forward Publishing Limited
25 Cross Street, Leamington Spa, CV32 4PX   Tel: 01926 420046   www.practicalpreschool.com
© Step Forward Publishing Limited 2001

Planning for Learning through Summer   ISBN: 1-902438-46-9

MAKING PLANS

WHY PLAN?

The purpose of planning is to make sure that all children enjoy a broad and balanced curriculum. All planning should be useful. Plans are working documents which you spend time preparing, but which should later repay your efforts. Try to be concise. This will help you in finding information quickly when you need it.

LONG-TERM PLANS

Preparing a long-term plan, which maps out the curriculum during a year or even two, will help you to ensure that you are providing a variety of activities and are meeting the statutory requirements of the *Curriculum Guidance for the Foundation Stage* (2000).

Your long-term plan need not be detailed. Divide the time period over which you are planning into fairly equal sections, such as half terms. Choose a topic for each section. Young children benefit from making links between the new ideas they encounter so as you select each topic, think about the time of year in which you plan to do it. A topic about minibeasts will not be very successful in November!

Although each topic will address all the learning areas, some could focus on a specific area. For example, a topic on Summer would lend itself well to activities relating to knowledge and understanding of the living world. Another topic might particularly encourage the appreciation of stories. Try to make sure that you provide a variety of topics in your long-term plans.

Autumn 1	All about me
Autumn 2	Colour
	Christmas
Spring 1	Nursery rhymes
Spring 2	Toys
Summer 1	Minibeasts
Summer 2	Summer

MEDIUM-TERM PLANS

Medium-term plans will outline the contents of a topic in a little more detail. One way to start this process is by brainstorming on a large piece of paper. Work with your team writing down all the activities you can think of which are relevant to the topic. As you do this it may become clear that some activities go well together. Think about dividing them into themes. The topic of Summer, for example, has themes such as summer fruits and flowers, sunny week, at the seaside, summer holidays and sports day.

At this stage it is helpful to make a chart. Write the theme ideas down the side of the chart and put a different area of learning at the top of each column. Now you can insert your brainstormed ideas and will quickly see where there are gaps. As you complete the chart take account of children's earlier experiences and provide opportunities for them to progress.

Refer back to the *Curriculum Guidance for the Foundation Stage* (2000) and check that you have addressed as many different aspects as you can. Once all your medium-term plans are complete make sure that there are no neglected areas.

MAKING PLANS

DAY-TO-DAY PLANS

The plans you make for each day will outline aspects such as:

- resources needed;
- the way in which you might introduce activities;
- the organisation of adult help;
- size of the group;
- timing.

Identify the learning which each activity is intended to promote. Make a note of any assessments or observations that you are likely to carry out. On your plans make notes of which activities were particularly successful, or any changes you would make another time.

A FINAL NOTE

Planning should be seen as flexible. Not all groups meet every day, and not all children attend every day. Any part of the plan can be used independently, stretched over a longer period or condensed to meet the needs of any group. You will almost certainly adapt the activities as children respond to them in different ways and bring their own ideas, interests and enthusiasms. Be prepared to be flexible over timing as some ideas prove more popular than others. The important thing is to ensure that the children are provided with a varied and enjoyable curriculum which meets their individual developing needs.

USING THE BOOK

- Collect or prepare suggested resources as listed on page 21.

- Read the section which outlines links to the Early Learning Goals (pages 4 - 7) and explains the rationale for the topic of Summer.

- For each weekly theme, two activities are described in detail as examples to help you in your planning and preparation. Key vocabulary, questions and learning opportunities are identified.

- The skills chart on page 23 will help you to see at a glance which aspects of children's development are being addressed as a focus each week.

- As children take part in the Summer topic activities, their learning will progress. 'Collecting evidence' on page 22 explains how you might monitor children's achievements.

- Find out on page 20 how the topic can be brought together in a grand finale involving parents, children and friends.

- There is additional material to support the working partnership of families and children in the form of a 'Home links' page, and a parent's page at the back of the book.

It is important to appreciate that the ideas presented in this book will only be a part of your planning. Many activities which will be taking place as routine in your group may not be mentioned. For example, it is assumed that sand, dough, water, puzzles, floor toys and large scale apparatus are part of the ongoing pre-school experience. Many groups will also be able to provide access to computers and other aspects of information and communication technology. Role play areas, stories, rhymes and singing, and group discussion times are similarly assumed to be happening in each week although they may not be a focus for described activities.

USING THE EARLY LEARNING GOALS

Having decided on your topic and made your medium-term plans you can use the Early Learning Goals to highlight the key learning opportunities your activities will address. The goals are split into six areas: Personal, Social and Emotional Development; Communication, Language and Literacy; Mathematical Development; Knowledge and Understanding of the World; Physical Development and Creative Development. Do not expect each of your topics to cover every goal but your long-term plans should allow for all of them to be addressed by the time a child enters Year 1.

The following section highlights parts of the *Curriculum Guidance for the Foundation Stage* (2000) in point form to show what children are expected to be able to do in each area of learning by the time they enter Year 1. These points will be used throughout this book to show how activities for a topic on Summer link to these expectations. For example, Personal, Social and Emotional Development point 9 is 'understand what is right, what is wrong and why'. Activities suggested which provide the opportunity for children to do this will have the reference PS9. This will enable you to see which parts of the Early Learning Goals are covered in a given week and plan for areas to be revisited and developed.

In addition you can ensure that activities offer variety in the outcomes to be encountered. Often a similar activity may be carried out to achieve different outcomes. For example, children can play with bats and balls to develop motor skills and co-ordination. At the same time they may be learning to play collaboratively, to take turns and to be aware of space and safety.

It is important, therefore, that activities have clearly defined learning outcomes so that these may be emphasised during the activity and for recording purposes.

PERSONAL, SOCIAL AND EMOTIONAL DEVELOPMENT (PS)

This area of learning covers important aspects of development which affect the way children learn, behave and relate to others.

By the end of the Foundation Stage, most children will:

PS1   continue to be interested, excited and motivated to learn

PS2   be confident to try new activities, initiate ideas and speak in a familiar group

PS3   maintain attention, concentrate, and sit quietly when appropriate

PS4   have a developing awareness of their own needs, views and feelings and be sensitive to the needs, views and feelings of others

PS5   have a developing respect for their own cultures and beliefs and those of other people

PS6   respond to significant experiences, showing a range of feelings when appropriate

PS7   form good relationships with adults and peers

PS8   work as part of a group or class, taking turns and sharing fairly, understanding that there need to be agreed values and codes of behaviour for groups of people, including adults and children, to work together harmoniously

PS9   understand what is right, what is wrong, and why

PS10 dress and undress independently and manage their own personal hygiene

PS11 select and use activities and resources independently

PS12 consider the consequences of their words and actions for themselves and others

PS13 understand that people have different needs, views, cultures and beliefs, that need to be treated with respect

PS14 understand that they can expect others to treat their needs, views, cultures and beliefs with respect

The topic of Summer provides valuable opportunities for children to show sensitivity to their surroundings, to work collaboratively and to express feelings in response to natural objects. As children become more aware of the changes which take place in Summer they have the chance to explore new learning and develop ideas. In addition, many of the outcomes for Personal, Social and Emotional Development will develop as a natural result of activities in other key areas.
For example, when children play games within Physical Development they will also have the opportunity to further PS8.

COMMUNICATION, LANGUAGE AND LITERACY (L)

The objectives set out in the *National Literacy Strategy: Framework for Teaching* for the reception year are in line with these goals. By the end of the Foundation Stage, most children will be able to:

L1 enjoy listening to and using spoken and written language, and readily turn to it in their play and learning

L2 explore and experiment with sounds, words and texts

L3 listen with enjoyment and respond to stories, songs and other music, rhymes and poems and make up their own stories, songs, rhymes and poems

L4 use language to imagine and recreate roles and experiences

L5 use talk to organise, sequence and clarify thinking, ideas, feelings and events

L6 sustain attentive listening, responding to what they have heard by relevant comments, questions or actions

L7 interact with others, negotiating plans and activities and taking turns in conversation

L8 extend their vocabulary, exploring the meaning and sounds of new words

L9 retell narratives in the correct sequence, drawing on the language patterns of stories

L10 speak clearly and audibly with confidence and control and show awareness of the listener, for example by their use of conventions such as greetings, 'please' and 'thank you'

L11 hear and say initial and final sounds in words, and short vowel sounds within words

L12 link sounds to letters, naming and sounding the letters of the alphabet

L13 read a range of familiar and common words and simple sentences independently

L14 show an understanding of the elements of stories, such as main character, sequence of events, and openings, and how information can be found in non-fiction texts to answer questions about where, who, why and how

L15 know that print carries meaning and, in English, is read from left to right and top to bottom

L16 attempt writing for various purposes, using features of different forms such as lists, stories and instructions

L17 write their own names, labels and captions, and begin to form sentences, sometimes using punctuation

L18 use their phonic knowledge to write simple regular words and make phonetically plausible attempts at more complex words

L19 use a pencil and hold it effectively to form recognisable letters, most of which are correctly formed

The activities suggested for the theme of Summer include several in which children describe observations and events, reinforcing and extending their vocabulary. There are opportunities for role play as children respond to sounds, stories, poems and ideas. Creating a travel agent role play area will allow children to use their imaginations. Throughout the topic opportunities are described in which children explore the sounds of words and see some of their ideas recorded in both pictures and print.

MATHEMATICAL DEVELOPMENT (M)

The key objectives in the *National Numeracy Strategy: Framework for Teaching* for the reception year are in line with these goals. By the end of the Foundation Stage, most children will be able to:

M1 say and use number names in order in familiar contexts

M2 count reliably up to ten everyday objects

M3 recognise numerals 1 to 9

M4 use language such as 'more' or 'less' to compare two numbers

M5 in practical activities and discussion begin to use the vocabulary involved in adding and subtracting

M6 find one more or one less than a number from one to ten

M7 begin to relate addition to combining two groups of objects and subtraction to 'taking away'

M8 talk about, recognise and recreate simple patterns

M9 use language such as 'circle' or 'bigger' to describe the shape and size of solids and flat shapes

M10 use everyday words to describe position

M11 use developing mathematical ideas and methods to solve practical problems

M12 use language such as 'greater', 'smaller', 'heavier' or 'lighter' to compare quantities

The theme of Summer provides a meaningful context for mathematical activities which are closely linked to everyday experiences. Natural materials such as flowers and fruits provide opportunities for children to sort by size, colour and shape. Using these materials in slightly different ways encourages children to develop comparative and positional language. Simple activities, such as ordering a row of flowers by size, provide a wealth of language opportunities as well as a context for counting. Daisies can also be used as a non-standard unit for measuring length.

KNOWLEDGE AND UNDERSTANDING OF THE WORLD (K)

By the end of the Foundation Stage most children will be able to:

K1 investigate objects and materials by using all of their senses as appropriate

K2 find out about, and identify, some features of living things, objects and events they observe

K3 look closely at similarities, differences, patterns and change

K4 ask questions about why things happen and how things work

K5 build and construct with a wide range of objects, selecting appropriate resources, and adapting their work where necessary

K6 select tools and techniques they need to shape, assemble and join the materials they are using

K7 find out about and identify the uses of everyday technology and use information and communication technology and programmable toys to support their learning

K8 find out about past and present events in their own lives, and in those of their families and other people they know

K9 observe, find out about and identify features in the place they live and the natural world

K10 begin to know about their own cultures and beliefs and those of other people

K11 find out about their environment, and talk about those features they like and dislike

The topic of Summer provides opportunities to help children experience K2, 3, 4 and 9. In addition they will touch on K5, 6 and 11. For example, as children go on a walk to detect signs of Summer they will also talk about where they live and the local environment. When making marble minibeasts they will select resources.

PHYSICAL DEVELOPMENT (PD)

By the end of the Foundation Stage most children will be able to:

PD1 move with confidence, imagination and in safety

PD2 move with control and co-ordination

PD3 show awareness of space, of themselves and of others

PD4 recognise the importance of keeping healthy and those things which contribute to this

PD5 recognise the changes that happen to their bodies when they are active

PD6 use a range of small and large equipment

PD7 travel around, under, over and through balancing and climbing equipment

PD8 handle tools, objects, construction and malleable materials safely and with increasing control

Activities such as moving marble minibeasts or playing with bats and balls will offer experience of PD6. Through the activities associated with the sports day children can develop control and coordination while also having the opportunity to work both collaboratively and independently. Children will become aware of the restriction of space and the needs of others by playing whole group games.

CREATIVE DEVELOPMENT (C)

By the end of the Foundation Stage, most children will be able to:

C1 explore colour, texture, shape, form and space in two or three dimensions

C2 recognise and explore how sounds can be changed, sing simple songs from memory, recognise repeated sounds and sound patterns and match movements to music

C3 respond in a variety of ways to what they see, hear, smell, touch and feel

C4 use their imagination in art and design, music, dance, imaginative and role play and stories

C5 express and communicate their ideas, thoughts and feelings by using a widening range of materials, suitable tools, imaginative and role play, movement, designing and making, and a variety of songs and musical instruments

During this topic children will experience working with a variety of materials as they make models, such as making a model caravan in the summer holiday week, and explore a range of art and craft activities. Poetry and stories are used to inspire imaginative responses, for example travelling on a 'magic carpet' to imaginary or real holiday destinations.

Week 1

DETECTING SUMMER

PERSONAL, SOCIAL AND EMOTIONAL DEVELOPMENT

- Go on a walk to detect signs of the Summer. Before you go, talk about the importance of staying together, listening to instructions and being sensitive to the environment. (PS4, 8)

- Use a camera to record your walk. When the photographs are developed the children can work collaboratively to make a large book about the walk. (PS8)

COMMUNICATION, LANGUAGE AND LITERACY

- Encourage children to talk about the things they like to do in the Summer. Look at pictures of people outside in the Summer. Talk about the clothes people wear and what they are doing. (L5, 6, 7)

- Start to build a word bank of Summer words. Scribe words suggested by the children on large pieces of card or stiff paper (for example, ice-cream, sun, hot, seaside). Ask children to draw pictures by the words to illustrate them. (L2, 16)

MATHEMATICAL DEVELOPMENT

- Make ladybirds by painting small pebbles or red plastic lids from plastic milk bottles. Vary the number of dots on the ladybirds from one to six. Play simple dice and estimation games (see activity opposite). (M1, 2, 3)

- Show the children a large, safe thermometer, such as those from educational suppliers. Talk about how thermometers are used to measure how hot or cold something is. Introduce the word 'temperature'. Link to experiences children may

have had in having their temperature taken. Show how the thermometer has numbers on it, and that the bigger the number is, the hotter the temperature. What is the temperature of the air in the room? (M3)

KNOWLEDGE AND UNDERSTANDING OF THE WORLD

- Go on a minibeast hunt, encouraging children to look closely in small places, such as under a stone. Talk about why they need to be careful as they search. Explain that they are like giants in the world of tiny creatures and any disturbance, especially handling, should be avoided. (K1, 2, 3)

- Begin a sunny day chart to talk about in Week 3. Ask children each day how hot or sunny it is. Record this with sunny faces. If it's very hot, use either more suns or vary the size of the sun. (K3)

PHYSICAL DEVELOPMENT

- Make marble minibeasts and use them to go round card tracks (see activity opposite). (PD6, 8)

- Enjoy playing with bats and balls. (PD6)

CREATIVE DEVELOPMENT

- Encourage children to think about the sounds they hear during the Summer: lawn mowers, ice-cream vans, insects buzzing, birds singing, sea sounds or perhaps even a thunderstorm. Recreate these sounds using percussion instruments and body sounds. (C1, 3)

- Provide the children with large sheets of paper, brushes, paint or bright pastels and encourage them to make a picture of themselves carrying out a favourite summertime activity. (C1, 4, 5)

ACTIVITY: Ladybird games

Learning opportunity: Counting to six.

Early Learning Goal: Mathematical Development. Children will be able to recognise and use numbers to six.

Resources: 24 ladybirds made from red plastic milk bottle lids or painted pebbles (four ladybirds with one dot, four with two dots, and so on); four A4-sized leaves made from green felt; a dice numbered one to six; a dice numbered 0, 1, 1, 2, 2, 3.

Organisation: two to four children seated at a small table or comfortably on the floor.

Key vocabulary: How many...? Count, ladybird, leaf, one, two, three, four, five, six.

WHAT TO DO:

Show the children the ladybirds. Encourage them to work together to sort them into sets according to the number of spots. Ask children how many are in each set. Explain the rules and play one of the games below.

Give each child a leaf. Use the 0 to 3 dice. Check that children recognise and understand the numbers. In turn children shake the dice, pick up the number of ladybirds and place them on a leaf.

Give each child a leaf. Use the 1 to 6 dice. In turn children shake the dice and collect a ladybird with the same number of spots. The aim is to collect one for each number one to six. If children throw a number they have already collected they do not pick up a ladybird.

Put out six ladybirds. Ask children to count them. Spread them out. Ask how many there are. Count to show there are still six. Ask children to close their eyes. Take two of the ladybirds and hide them under a leaf. Ask the children to open their eyes and say how many are hiding. Help the children to count the four they can see and to work out that two are under the leaf. Repeat by hiding other numbers.

ACTIVITY: Marble minibeasts

Learning opportunity: Using scissors with control and regard for safety. Controlling speed and direction of marble minibeasts through a maze.

Early Learning Goal: Physical Development. Children will be able to handle small equipment and tools safely and with control.

Resources: A ready-made marble minibeast; for each child a plastic drinks bottle lid; a marble; a piece of card about 10 x 10cm; a pair of scissors; felt pens or crayons; double-sided sticky tape; a pre-drawn maze on stiff A4 card.

Organisation: Up to six children seated around a table.

Key vocabulary: Minibeast, names for minibeasts made by the children.

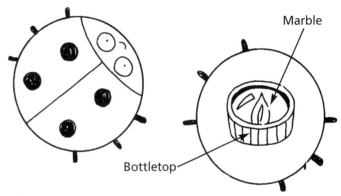

Minibeast cut out of card and coloured with crayons

Underside of card ladybird

Marble

Bottletop

WHAT TO DO:

Let the children look at the ready-made minibeast. Show them how it is made and suggest they make their own. A minibeast is cut from card and stuck to the top of the lid with sticky tape. Place a marble under the lid and invite children to take their creatures for walks.

Introduce children to the mazes - a simple route drawn on card with a start and finish. Show how the minibeasts can be steered along the routes. Encourage children to persevere!

DISPLAY

Start a Summer wall display by making a background of grassy green with occasional sponge printed leafy trees. As the topic progresses children will enjoy adding cut-outs of themselves carrying out various activities, or can add items which will personalise the display to your area. Examples might include a feature of a local park, familiar characters or buildings. Display the children's illustrations of Summer activities, with suitable captions dictated by the children.

Week 2

SUMMER FRUITS

PERSONAL, SOCIAL AND EMOTIONAL DEVELOPMENT

- Having first checked that no child has a fruit allergy, show children a bowl containing a selection of summer fruits. Talk about the types of fruits children like to eat and why. Explain that it is healthy to eat fruit. At snack time remind children to wash their hands and then eat pieces of apple. (PS1, 6, 10)

- Talk about the dangers of picking fruits without adult supervision. Even familiar fruits growing in gardens can hide hidden dangers, such as wasps later in the summer. (PS1, 9)

COMMUNICATION, LANGUAGE AND LITERACY

- Set up the role play area as a fruit and flower market stall. Encourage children to take it in turns to be traders and customers and to talk about the reasons for buying the produce. (L4)

- Use the role play area as the stimulus for children to make summer shopping lists in words and/or pictures. (L16)

- Make a collection of words which can be used to describe fruits. Start by looking at the shape of the fruit. Talk about the colour and texture of the outside, and finally break or cut open the fruit to see the inside. Allow the children to touch and smell the fruit before dividing it into tiny pieces for tasting. (L4, 8)

MATHEMATICAL DEVELOPMENT

- Sort pips, fruits or pictures of fruits into sets by shape, type or colour. Use the same items to make sets of given numbers: 'Can you make sets of four?' (M2, 4)

- Use the banana finger rhyme (see activity opposite) or adapt familiar ones for the Summer fruit theme. (M1, 2)

- As you carry out the fruit printing activity talk about halving the fruit or cutting it into quarters. As the children print encourage the use of repeating patterns. (M8)

KNOWLEDGE AND UNDERSTANDING OF THE WORLD

- Use fruit purees sold as baby foods to carry out a 'taste and try' activity. Can children identify the different fruit flavours? (Baby foods are amongst the safest possible to use for this type of activity but check group allergy records before any tasting activity.) (K1, 3)

- Make bookmarks from pressed flowers. (K1, 2, 3)

PHYSICAL DEVELOPMENT

- With the children sitting in a circle, go around the group allocating the name of a fruit to each child. Use a repeating selection such as apple, pear, orange, lemon, apple . . . so that there are several children in each fruit group. Explain to the children that you are going to make up a story, and that each time their fruit is mentioned they are going to do a particular action, for example, apples - clap, pears -stand up. Now make up a story, perhaps about a trip to a fruit market, and gradually speed up the frequency with which different fruits are mentioned! (PD2)

- Sing action rhymes with a fruit theme, such as 'Here is the tree with leaves so green' (This Little Puffin - see Resources, page 21). (PD1)

CREATIVE DEVELOPMENT

- Use pastels and chalks to make close observational pictures of fruits. Encourage children to match colours accurately. Provide each child with a piece of scrap paper for trying out colours. Show children how a small piece of sponge can be used to smudge chalks and pastels to mix the colours. (C5)

- Print with pieces of fruit (see activity opposite). (C1)

ACTIVITY : Fruit printing

Learning opportunity: Using a variety of materials for printing.

Early Learning Goal: Creative Development. Children will be able to explore texture, shape, form and space in two or three dimensions.

Resources: Safe fruit knife, cutting board, sugar paper, ready mixed or thick powder paints, saucers, sponges, variety of fruits such as lemon, apple, pear, orange, star fruit (avoid stoned or very soft fruits).

Organisation: Children working in a small group at a table. It is often more comfortable for small children to print from a standing position.

Key vocabulary: Names of fruits being used, colours of the fruits.

WHAT TO DO:

Give children a whole fruit to handle, reinforcing vocabulary which describes its colour, texture, shape. Ask the children to tell you what they think is inside the fruit. Remind them about fruits they have eaten to help them. Cut through the fruit and compare with the children's ideas.

For each colour of paint you wish to use, prepare a sponge by covering it in paint and placing it in a saucer. Show the children how to press their cut fruit onto a sponge before pressing it onto their paper. Demonstrate how to hold the fruit firmly and steadily to avoid a smudged print.

Talk about repeating patterns and designs. Would the print be the same if the fruit was cut in a different way?

ACTIVITY: The banana counting rhyme

Learning opportunity: Developing familiarity with numbers to five.

Early Learning Goal: Mathematical Development. Children will be able to say and use number names in order in familiar contexts and count reliably everyday objects.

Resources: None.

Organisation: Whole group.

Key vocabulary: One, two, three, four, five.

WHAT TO DO:

Use carpet or circle time to learn and enjoy this rhyme. After each verse count the fingers being held up to reinforce number awareness.

5 bananas in a bunch *Hold up 5 fingers*
I break one off to have for lunch, *Mime undoing the banana and biting*
I eat up my banana, and I throw the skin away *Mime throwing skin in bin*
4 bananas left for another sunny day. *Hold up 4 fingers*

Last verse
1 banana from my bunch
I pick it up to have for lunch.................

DISPLAY

Display the fruit printing work with examples of the fruits used to make them. Can children or visitors tell which fruit was used to make each print?

Week 3
SUMMER FLOWERS

PERSONAL, SOCIAL AND EMOTIONAL DEVELOPMENT

- Talk about the occasions on which flowers are given as gifts. Show children how to make paper flowers which they can give to a chosen person as a thank-you. (PS4)

- Read the story 'My naughty little sister is very sorry' from *My Naughty Little Sister's Friends* (see Resources, page 21). Discuss the feelings of both the little sister and the neighbour from whose garden she picked the flower. (PS4, 9)

COMMUNICATION, LANGUAGE AND LITERACY

- Involve the children in making a flower alphabet display, using flower books and garden catalogues. (L12)

- Sing or recite nursery rhymes with a flower or plant theme; 'Lavender's Blue' 'Mary, Mary Quite Contrary' or 'I had a Little Nut Tree'. (L3, 10)

- Read the story of *Titch* (see Resources). Use the story to introduce and develop comparative language relating to size. (L3)

MATHEMATICAL DEVELOPMENT

- Use plant catalogues for children to make sets of flowers. For example, ask children to cut out three orange flowers, five pink flowers and one yellow. Stick the flowers in sets. Introduce early addition by asking more able children to count the flowers. (M2, 4, 5)

- Make daisy counting chains (see activity opposite). (M2)

- Cut out petal shapes in a variety of colours which children arrange around yellow flower centres. Introduce ideas of pattern as children place petals in alternate colours or make repeating patterns. Can the children recognise and continue a pattern which you begin? (M8)

PHYSICAL DEVELOPMENT

- Draw a set of flower-shaped targets on the ground outside, using playground chalk. Alternatively draw them on the sides of large boxes which can be weighted to keep them stable. Use bean bags to practise throwing and aiming. (PD6)

- Play ring games with a flowery theme, such as 'Ring a ring o' roses', 'Here we go round the mulberry bush' and 'In and out the dusky bluebells'.(PD1)

KNOWLEDGE AND UNDERSTANDING OF THE WORLD

- Talk to the children about the needs of growing plants. What happens to cut flowers if they are left out of water? Place some white flowers in a mixture of water and food colouring and leave overnight. What do the children notice? (K2, 3, 9)

- Reinforce the names of the parts of a flower - petals, leaves and stem. Explain that although these can be different colours and shapes in different plants, the names of the parts stay the same. (K2, 3)

- Talk about the way in which plants are often grown in compost. Replace the sand in the sand tray with compost (bought from a garden centre rather than from your garden, though you can explain how compost can be made), and provide sieves, trowels and plastic plant pots as tools. Encourage the children to explore the texture and properties of the compost as they play. (K1,3)

- Make pressed flower bookmarks (see activity opposite). (K2, 3)

CREATIVE DEVELOPMENT

- Use finger paints to make the petals and leaves in daisy pictures. (C1)

- Fold circles of tissue paper in half and then in half again. Using safe tapestry needles show the children how to thread these onto a length of shearing elastic, taking the needle through the point of the folded tissue each time. Once the threading is complete, tie the ends of the elastic together and open out all the folded tissue circles to make a flower garland, bracelet or anklet. (C5)

- Give each child a box with one face removed, to leave a tray-like container. Half fill with compost. Provide a selection of tiny twigs and flowers, such as daisies or buttercups, and let children to create their own miniature gardens. Have modelling materials to hand as some children will enjoy making foil ponds, or lolly-stick fences. (C5)

- Use pasta to make a garden collage. To colour the pasta before use, place diluted food colouring in a small bowl. Add a handful of raw pasta and mix. Drain, and spread the pasta on a baking sheet covered in non-stick parchment. Dry in a slightly warm oven. (C1, 5)

ACTIVITY: Daisy chains

Learning opportunity: Using paper flowers as a context for counting.

Early Learning Goal: Mathematical Development. Children will be able to count reliably up to ten everyday objects.

Resources: Prepared white daisy shapes, made by folding circles of white paper, cutting a petal outline and then opening out. Yellow or orange paper circles for the centres of the flowers. Strips of green paper, crepe paper or ribbon.

Organisation: Children working in small groups with an adult.

WHAT TO DO:

Show the children how to make white daisy flower shapes using the pre-cut shapes, and adding chosen centres.

Demonstrate how to glue the daisies to a strip of green paper, crepe or ribbon which can be hung vertically to make pretend daisy chains.

Count the daisies with the children and support the more able in writing an appropriate numeral in the centre of each flower to make a daisy counting line.

ACTIVITY: Pressed-flower bookmarks

Learning opportunity: Observing features of flowers.

Early Learning Goal: Knowledge and understanding of the world. Children will be able to find out about and identify features of living things. They will look closely at similarities and differences.

Resources: PVA glue; stiff black card cut into bookmarks (about 21cm x 6cm); paper kitchen towel; sticky-back plastic; flowers to press; heavy books; a pre-made bookmark; a pen.

Organisation: Small group.

Key vocabulary: Five, flower, names of flowers used.

WHAT TO DO:

Show children the pre-made bookmark. Explain that they are going to make one as a present their family (possibly for Fathers' Day). Show how flowers can be pressed by laying them in a piece of folded paper kitchen towel then placed in a heavy book. If possible, go to an area where children may pick flowers. Explain that flowers can only be picked where permission is given to do so.

Talk about the names of the plants and the colours. Ask children to pick five which look good together. Inside, help children to press their flowers. Write the child's name on the kitchen towel.

About a week later, remove the flowers from the books and help children to stick them with minimal glue on the black card. Once stuck an adult should cover the bookmark with clear sticky-back plastic or laminate it.

DISPLAY

Make a collection of household objects, fabrics or wrapping papers which have a floral design. Give the display a title such as 'Flowers all around us' and invite children to bring in objects (with parental permission) to contribute to the display.

Week 4

SUNNY WEEK

PERSONAL, SOCIAL AND EMOTIONAL DEVELOPMENT

- Talk about sun safety. Show the children a selection of sun hats and sunscreen lotions. Make posters to encourage people to protect themselves from the sun. Encourage children to take responsibility for themselves by wearing hats and keeping in the shade. (PS5, 8)

- Talk about droughts and countries where it is always hot. Talk about ways we can save water such as not leaving the tap running when we clean our teeth. (PS4)

COMMUNICATION, LANGUAGE AND LITERACY

- Write a group poem about the sun. Display the poem in a big book. (L7, 17)

- Show the children pictures of children on a sunny day. Talk about the sequence of events as a child wakes and dresses on a sunny morning. (L2, 4, 5)

- Play a version of the 'I went shopping' game. Children sit in a circle. The first child starts the story by saying 'I woke up one sunny day and I . .' choosing a suitable activity with which to complete the sentence. The second child repeats the opening phrase and activity, and then adds their own. The game progresses around the group, each child adding their own activity to the list. Encourage all the children to help each other to remember the list in their turn. (L1, 6)

MATHEMATICAL DEVELOPMENT

- Make paper fans from concertina folded A4 paper. Colour the fan with repeating patterns. (M8)

- Talk about the sun making shadows and then play a shadow guessing game. You will need a collection of familiar objects, such as a teddy, a toy car, a fork or a cup. Make a simple screen from a large piece of white paper. Ask a child or adult helper to hold the screen slightly in front of you. Hold one of the objects between yourself and the screen. Using the other hand, shine a torch onto the object, casting a shadow onto the screen. Can the children guess the mystery objects from their shadows? (M9, 10)

KNOWLEDGE AND UNDERSTANDING OF THE WORLD

- Talk about the differences between day time and night time. (Bear in mind that children who live in cities may have little experience of starry skies.) Introduce vocabulary such as morning, afternoon, evening, last night, yesterday. (K3)

- On a sunny day go outside to investigate shadows. Can the children escape from their shadows? Does it always copy movements exactly? Can the children jump over their shadows? (K2, 3, 4, 9)

- Allow the children to take objects outside to investigate shadows. Interesting shadow makers include objects with holes in them, such as sieves, colanders, or plant pots. How does the shadow change as the object is turned? (K2, 3, 4, 9)

- Make a suncatcher (see activity opposite). (K2, 4, 5)

PHYSICAL DEVELOPMENT

- Remind the children about the importance of staying in the shade on a hot, sunny day. What types of activities do the children enjoy playing in the shade? Invite a parent or grandparent into the group who is able to demonstrate some of the playground games of skill which they enjoyed as children: marbles, jacks or tiddly winks. (PD2, 6)

- Play musical shadows. Take a musical instrument outside and explain to the children that they are going to move around to the sound of the instrument. When the instrument stops, you will tell them what sort of shadow to make, for example a tall shadow, a small shadow, a spiky shadow or a wide shadow. (PD1, 2)

CREATIVE DEVELOPMENT

- Make a sunshine collage. Provide wool, paper scraps and curls, dyed pasta or woodshavings, fabric scraps and so on, all in bright reds, yellows and oranges. Stick them on to round shapes pre-cut from yellow paper or card. (C1)

- Cut out pictures from greetings cards and mount them on straws to make simple shadow puppets. Provide a screen to either take outside in the sunshine, or to use with a torch indoors. (C4)

ACTIVITY: Making a suncatcher

Learning opportunity: Exploring aspects of colour and transparency.

Early Learning Goal: Knowledge and Understanding of the World. Children will be able to find out about and identify features of objects.

Resources: Small boxes (mini cereal boxes), coloured cellophane, scissors, sticky tape or glue, string.

Organisation: Children working in small groups at a table.

Key vocabulary: hole, the colours of the cellophane.

WHAT TO DO:

Help each child to cut out very large holes in the four sides of a small box. Leave the top and bottom intact.

Cover the holes with coloured cellophane. Encourage the use of a different colour in covering each hole. Accuracy is not crucial.

Finally, tape a length of string to the top of the box so that it can be hung in front of a window at child height.

As the box turns in the sunshine the children can spot the colours which they see. Sometimes a coloured pattern will be seen on a wall or the floor.

ACTIVITY: Write a sunny poem for a big book

Learning opportunity: Using descriptive words. Collaborating to make a big book.

Early Learning Goal: Communication, Language and Literacy. Children will be able to interact with others, negotiating plans and activities and taking turns in conversation. They will write their own names and begin to form simple sentences.

Resources: Suns cut from large paper; pencils and crayons; large picture or poster of people outside on a sunny day (see Resources).

Organisation: Whole group introduction, small groups of up to eight children for the writing and drawing.

Key vocabulary: Sun, sunny.

WHAT TO DO:

Introduction: Show the group a large picture of people on a sunny day. Talk about the types of activities people are doing. What do children do when it is sunny? Show the group the cut-out suns. Explain that together they are going to make a book about what children do on sunny days. Break up into small groups, each with an adult.

Small group development: Play a game in which each child completes the sentence 'When it is sunny (child's name) likes to . . .' Encourage children to use descriptive words, for example, 'When it is sunny Jonathan likes to sit in icy water in his paddling pool'. After each child has had a go, talk about the responses. Were any similar? Can one child recall another's sentence? Give each child a sun and ask them to draw a picture of what they do when it is sunny. For each child scribe their sentence or help them to overwrite/underwrite/copy it. When all are finished, read the whole 'poem' back to the group.

When all small groups have finished their suns, mount them in a big book and ask children who are able to write their name on the cover. Display the book in the reading area for all to share and enjoy.

Instead of making a big book, pictures can be drawn on smaller suns cut from A4 card. The sentence can then be written on the back and the suns hung from the ceiling at a level where children can look at or read them.

DISPLAY

Make a display of the sunshine collages together with some items of hot weather wear, such as sunglasses, swimming clothes, beach towel and a sunshade. If you have made card suns, hang them above the display.

Week 5

SUMMER HOLIDAYS

PERSONAL, SOCIAL AND EMOTIONAL DEVELOPMENT

- Tell the children a story about a child who goes on a day visit and behaves badly. Perhaps in the end she could wake to find it was a dream which gives her the chance to behave perfectly on the real outing! Use the story as the basis for a discussion about how to behave in new places and the importance of children staying with the adult taking them. (PS3, 8, 9)

- Talk to the children about the need for occasional breaks from work. Even if it is only a quiet sit down, everyone needs some time off! Suggest that they might give their mums or dads a short break by helping with a household chore, or playing quietly while they have a chat. (PS4)

COMMUNICATION, LANGUAGE AND LITERACY

- Play a holiday guessing game. Say to the children, 'These are the things I am going to pack - Can you guess where I am going?' Make up some lists which are fairly indicative of particular types of places: a swimsuit, sunglasses, large towel and sunshade, or a warm jacket, trousers, hat, gloves, boots and skis. Fantasy ideas might include: a space helmet and astronaut's suit, or a pirate's hat, map and spade. Allow children to join in by making their own lists for others to guess. (L1, 6, 10)

- Make a travel agency role play area. Provide a desk, telephone, paper and pencils, pretend tickets and leaflets. Ask for unwanted posters from travel agencies to go on the wall. Provide a role model by showing children how to browse through the leaflets and then book a holiday with the help of the agency assistant. How would you like to travel? For how long will you be away? (L1)

- Make postcards to send. Show the children a selection of holiday postcards. Draw attention to their features: a picture on one side, a space to write in, a space for an address and a space to stick a stamp. Provide children with postcard-sized pieces of card and see if they can design and make their own fantasy postcards. More able children may enjoy writing a simple message on the back and filling in their own addresses. (L15, 16, 17, 19)

MATHEMATICAL DEVELOPMENT

- Make a packing/number recognition game (see activity opposite). (M1, 3)

- How quickly can you pack? Make a timing game using a collection of a few suitable clothes or pieces of holiday equipment and a suitcase. In turn, children estimate how long it is going to take them to pack the case and then test their predictions. Use non-standard measures of time. How many times could other children sing a nursery rhyme during the packing or how many bricks could they stack? Make up rules for the packing, such as only one item to be packed at a time to make the game last longer. (M4, 11, 12)

KNOWLEDGE AND UNDERSTANDING OF THE WORLD

- Talk about all the different ways of travelling. Encourage children to describe their experiences of trains, buses, cars and perhaps planes or boats. Sing action songs to match each form of transport, such as 'Down at the station', 'The Wheels on the Bus', 'Aeroplanes, aeroplanes all in a row', 'Here is the sea, the wavy sea'. All these can be found in *This Little Puffin* (see Resources). (K9)

- Talk about places the children have visited. How were they different from their own familiar locality? Illustrate with postcards. (K9, 11)

PHYSICAL DEVELOPMENT

- Mime the events associated with preparing for a journey (packing clothes, preparing a picnic), travelling and arriving. Encourage children to describe their imaginary destination. (PD1)

- Make an obstacle course with each item representing an event on a journey, rather along the lines of 'Going on a Bear Hunt'. For example, the children could travel through a tunnel (play tunnel), over a mountain (climbing obstacle), between the trees (cones) and over the stepping stones to cross the river (mats). (PD2, 7)

CREATIVE DEVELOPMENT

- Sit with the children on a mat or carpet and explain to them that this is a magic carpet. It can take the children wherever they would like to go for a holiday. The places they choose could be places they know or exciting imaginary places such as a land of giants. Follow the children's ideas, talk them through the events happening as you take off on your great adventure. Closing eyes can help children to focus on imaginative thoughts. (C3)

- Make a model caravan - see activity opposite. (C5)

ACTIVITY: The suitcase game

Learning opportunity: Recognising and matching numbers.

Early Learning Goal: Mathematical Development. Children will be able to count reliably up to ten everyday objects. They will recognise numerals 1 to 9.

Resources: Prepared boards and pieces, dice.

Organisation: Up to four children at a time, depending on resources.

Key vocabulary: Numbers one to ten.

WHAT TO DO:

Prepare a game board for each child. This will take the form of a suitcase outline drawn onto card. Within the suitcase outline are the silhouette shapes of a pair of sandals, a sun hat, a pair of sunglasses, a pair of shorts, a T-shirt and a beach towel.

These items are also prepared as individual playing pieces, ideally mounted on card and laminated. Try to ensure that each piece matches its outline on the suitcase game board.

In addition each piece has a number on it.

Pair of sandals	1	Sun hat	2
Pair of sunglasses	3	Pair of shorts	4
T-shirt	5	Beach towel	6

Children collect the items in their cases by throwing the dice, counting the spots and collecting the piece with the appropriate number. If the game becomes slow to finish, encourage children to add to each other's boards as they win pieces they do not need themselves.

ACTIVITY: Making a caravan

Learning opportunity: Using a variety of materials within an imaginative context.

Early Learning Goal: Creative Development. Children will be able to express and communicate their ideas, thoughts and feelings by using a widening range of materials.

Resources: Shoe boxes, recycled modelling materials, additional materials (such as pipe-cleaners, lolly-sticks and fabric scraps), pre-cut card wheels, paint, brushes, scissors, glue, adhesive tape.

Organisation: Small group.

Key vocabulary: Caravan, house, wheels.

WHAT TO DO:

Ask the children if any of them have ever been in a caravan. What is a caravan like? Most children will have some understanding of the idea of a 'house on wheels'. Explain to the children that they are going to make their own model caravans.

Show the children how to use a shoe box as the main part of their caravan.

Provide a large selection of materials, such as small pieces of fabric, pieces of foil, card, small boxes such as matchboxes. Inside the shoe box they can use any materials they like to make the beds, tables, curtains and windows and so on.

Put the lids on the boxes and then the outside of the caravan can be painted. Finally, the cardboard wheels are glued into place.

DISPLAY

Display a collection of children's souvenirs of their holidays or days out.

Week 6

SPORTS DAY

PERSONAL, SOCIAL AND EMOTIONAL DEVELOPMENT

- Read *Sports Day* by Nick Butterworth and Mick Inkpen. Talk about sports days. Talk about races and what it feels like to win and to lose (see activity opposite). (PS4)

- Remind the children about sensible precautions to take in case the sports day is sunny. Discuss the importance of sun-hats and creams, spending time in the shade and having plenty to drink. (PS3, 9)

COMMUNICATION, LANGUAGE AND LITERACY

- Read the story *Dogger*, by Shirley Hughes (see Resources). Do any of the children have older brothers or sisters who have school sports days? Use the story to introduce some of the events which they might see at a sports day (L3, 5, 6).

- At your sports day, each child will receive a certificate to mark their taking part. Encourage each child to help in writing their name on a certificate and perhaps decorating it. (L17, 19)

- Through discussion, discover the sports with which children are familiar. Record the names of the sports on a chart and encourage the children to mime each sport as it is listed. (L6, 16)

MATHEMATICAL DEVELOPMENT

- Use the context of sports to introduce and reinforce the comparative language of speed: fast, faster, fastest; slow, slower and slowest. Use these words as children move around the room: clap, shake, nod, jump or play instruments. (M4)

- Races provide the opportunity to introduce ordinal numbers: first, second, third and so on. Illustrate these by enacting a toys' sports day with the children. Who do the children think would come first, second and third in each race? Encourage children to predict places in the Great Toy Car Grand Prix. Award rosettes to the winners of the teddy bear's race! (M1)

- Practise speedy movements and further develop a sense of time using sand timer activities. Set a series of challenges: How many beads can you thread before the sand runs through? How many times can you bounce a ball and catch it? (M11)

KNOWLEDGE AND UNDERSTANDING OF THE WORLD

- Talk about body parts and how joints move. Make card people with brass fasteners for arm and leg joints (see activity opposite). (K4)

- Encourage children to notice changes which happen in their bodies as they exercise. Encourage children to be aware of feeling hot and out of breath. Practise warming up, exercising and cooling down. (K3, 4)

PHYSICAL DEVELOPMENT

- Practise some of the activities for the sports day (see page 20). (PD1, 2)

- Sing action songs which concentrate on body movements such as: 'If you're happy and you know it', 'One finger one thumb keep moving', 'Head, shoulders, knees and toes'. (PD2)

CREATIVE DEVELOPMENT

- With the children sitting in a large space, play a guessing game in which you describe actions, clothes or equipment needed to play a particular sport. Once the children have guessed the sport they can begin to mime its actions. Give more clues until all the children are joining in. (C4)

- Encourage the children to help in decorating information posters about the sports day. (C5)

- Reinforce the language of speed through a blow-painting activity. Children start with a blob of runny paint placed on a paper using a dropper or teaspoon. They then blow the paint using a clean drinking straw. The straw should be held low down, almost parallel to the paper in order to blow the paint effectively. Use phrases such as 'The paint is going really fast now. It's slowing down. It's stopped.' (C1)

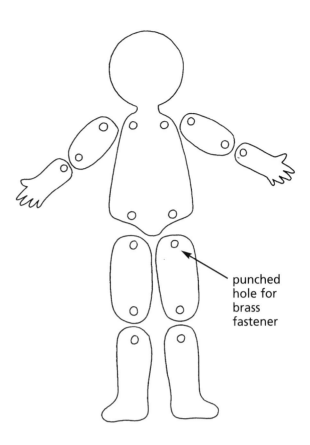

punched
hole for
brass
fastener

ACTIVITY: Sports day

Learning opportunity: Discussing how it feels to win and to lose and the importance of always trying to do your best.

Early Learning Goal: Personal, Social and Emotional Development. Children will have a developing awareness of their own needs, views and feelings and be sensitive to the needs, views and feelings of others.

Resources: *Sports Day* by Nick Butterworth and Mick Inkpen; flip chart.

Organisation: Whole group.

Key vocabulary: Race, sports day, win, lose.

WHAT TO DO:

Read *Sports Day* or a similar story about a sports day. Talk about the types of races and how the children in the book might have felt when they did well and when things did not go quite right.

Discuss how in races it does not matter if you come first or last, what is important is doing your best. Also talk about how to react if you play a game and win. Talk about being sensitive to others feelings.

Explain that they are going to have a sports day. Tell them there will be lots of races and games. Some will be like the ones in the story but others might be games the children have played during the year. Ask children to suggest games and races that they would like to do and to say why they think they would be good. Encourage children to talk about some stationary games (How many toy bricks can you stack with one hand in a given time?) as well as the more active races which involve running. Record suggestions on a flip chart.

ACTIVITY: Card people

Learning opportunity: Asking questions about body joints. Using brass fasteners to join pieces of card together.

Early Learning Goal: Knowledge and Understanding of the World. Children will be able to ask questions about how things work.

Resources: Display board with background as a playing field; an example of a completed body. For each child: pre-drawn body parts on card (see illustration); colouring pens and crayons; scissors; four brass fasteners.

Organisation: Whole group introduction, six children for making the bodies.

Key vocabulary: Elbow, shoulder, knee, hip, bend.

WHAT TO DO:

Whole group introduction: Ask for a volunteer to stand up. Point to the child's elbows, shoulders, knees and hips. Check that children know the names for these joints. Ask children why it is useful to have knees which bend. Talk about things we can do because they bend (kick a ball, sit cross-legged). Ask a child to walk round the room without bending their knees. How easy was it? Talk about other joints of the body which help us to move. Show the children the jointed card person. Explain that they are each going to make one to look like a child on sports day. Talk about the kind of clothes it should wear. Show children how brass fasteners can be used for shoulder, elbow, knee and hip joints.

Small group: Ask children to colour the body parts and to cut them out. Attach the arms and legs with brass fasteners.

DISPLAY

Children can place their completed sports person on the playing field display. Fasten the person to the board using staples through the neck and bottom thus allowing children to alter the positions of the arms and legs.

BRINGING IT ALL TOGETHER

INTRODUCING THE SPORTS DAY IDEA

Explain to the children that in a few days time the group is going to hold a sports day. Remind the children of the work they have already done about sports days, and encourage them to contribute their ideas about what such an event might involve.

Explain to the children that on their sports day, everyone is going to have a go at several activities, and everyone is going to be a winner!

During the sports day the children move around a circuit of small activities. Each one is a challenge of skill. Suggested ideas include:

- **The rope maze** Fold a very long skipping rope or washing line in half and lay it on the ground in such a way as to make a track which can be followed by children. Older children could be asked to roll a ball along the maze.

- **The balancing rope** This activity again starts with a rope laid on the ground, but this rope is used to form a single straight line. The children's challenge is to walk along the rope with feet at all times touching the rope. The skill is to keep the feet straight in front of each other, in what is essentially a balancing activity.

- **Target throwing** Make a simple target throwing challenge, such as throwing a bean bag into a bucket from a short distance.

- **The obstacle course** Make a mini obstacle course including, for example, hoops to climb through, stepping stones to cross, a held rope to crawl under and a plank on the ground to walk along.

- **Skittles** Use bought skittles, or make your own using washing-up liquid or plastic soft drinks bottles which can be decorated and slightly weighted.

- **The ball rolling slalom** Make a short slalom course by placing half a dozen cones in a spaced row. Children roll the ball in and out of the cones. This can be adapted as a steering activity if your group has ride-on toys.

Each activity will need to be manned by an adult (two in some cases). Children move around the activities in small groups, with a signal to move on given every few minutes. Each child taking part will need a prepared card with the name of each activity on it. As each activity is completed the card is ticked by the attending adult. Ensure that all supporting adults understand that this is not a competition for young children. Every child should receive as much support as they need to complete each station, including a little rule bending where necessary! Completion of the card earns a certificate, sticker, home-made rosette or tiny prize. (It is anticipated that every child with achieve this).

At this event there is unlikely to be any need for refreshment other than drinks and perhaps some biscuits. Some groups, however, may like to combine the event with a lunch or tea-time picnic, particularly if the weather is warm and sunny.

PREPARATIONS

Invite children to make suggestions about the types of activity which you might incorporate into your sports day event. Perhaps they have favourite activities they would like to include.

- **Invitations** Adult help will be vital to the success of this event. Support will be needed in looking after each event, serving refreshments and helping children to complete the challenges. Ask for help in a prepared letter which can be photocopied for parents and carers and pasted inside a piece of folded card. Involve children by asking them to decorate the outside of the cards. (Use the letter to remind parents and carers about the possible need for sun protection.)

  Children may like to invite younger brothers and sisters to join in the activities, or friends who do not normally attend the group. If so you will need to know numbers in advance so that enough recording passports and completion awards are available.

- **Accessories** Involve the children in: Choosing refreshment drinks. Writing their names on and decorating their personal recording passports which they will take with them around the events. Making flags or signs to name each activity station.

RESOURCES

RESOURCES TO COLLECT :

- A few magazines, colour supplements and travel brochures.
- Shopping catalogues with pictures of summer clothes and outdoor toys.
- Examples of summer fruits, vegetables and flowers.
- Fruit juices for making iced lollies - arrange for access to a freezer if necessary.
- Small hand-held puzzles.
- Sea shells and small, clean pebbles.
- Seasonal posters and pictures such as the Practical Pre-school Seasons Posters - Spring, Summer, Autumn, Winter.
- A large, safe thermometer from an educational supplier.

EVERYDAY RESOURCES:

- Boxes, large and small for modelling including shoe boxes and miniature cereal boxes.
- Papers and cards of different weights, colours and textures available such as sugar paper, corrugated card, silver and shiny papers.
- Selection of coloured cellophane or acetates.
- Different sized paint brushes from household brushes to thin brushes for delicate work and a variety of paint mixing containers.
- A variety of drawing and colouring pencils, crayons, pastels, charcoals, chalks.
- Small yoghurt or fromage frais pots and lolly-sticks.
- Table covers.
- Sand timers.

STORIES

Sports Day by Nick Butterworth and Mick Inkpen (Hodder Children's Books).

Maisy Goes Swimming by Lucy Cousins (Walker).

Oliver's Fruit Salad by Vivian French (Hodder Children's Books).

Dogger by Shirley Hughes (Red Fox).

Lucy and Tom at the Seaside by Shirley Hughes (Puffin).

Titch by Pat Hutchins (Red Fox).

The Giant Jam Sandwich by John Vernon Lord (Pan Books).

My Naughty Little Sister's Friends by Dorothy Edwards (Mammoth).

POEMS

First Verses compiled by John Foster (Oxford University Press).

This Little Puffin by Elizabeth Matterson (Puffin).

Out and About by Shirley Hughes (Walker).

Playtime Rhymes by Sally Gardner (Orion Children's Books).

Twinkle Twinkle Chocolate Bar compiled by John Foster (Oxford University Press).

COLLECTING EVIDENCE OF CHILDREN'S LEARNING

Monitoring children's development is an important task. Keeping a record of children's achievements will help you to see progress and will draw attention to those who are having difficulties for some reason. If a child needs additional professional help, such as speech therapy, your records will provide valuable evidence.

Records should be the result of collaboration between group leaders, parents and carers. Parents should be made aware of your record keeping policies when their child joins your group. Show them the type of records you are keeping and make sure they understand that they have an opportunity to contribute. As a general rule, your records should form an open document. Any parent should have access to records relating to his or her child. Take regular opportunities to talk to parents about children's progress. If you have formal discussions regarding children about whom you have particular concerns, a dated record of the main points should be kept.

KEEPING IT MANAGEABLE

Records should be helpful in informing group leaders, adult helpers and parents and always be for the benefit of the child. However, keeping records of every aspect of each child's development can become a difficult task. The sample shown will help to keep records manageable and useful. The golden rule is to keep them simple.

Observations will basically fall into three categories:

- **Spontaneous records:** Sometimes you will want to make a note of observations as they happen, for example, a child is heard counting cars accurately during a play activity, or is seen to play collaboratively for the first time.

- **Planned observations:** Sometimes you will plan to make observations of children's developing skills in their everyday activities. Using the learning opportunity identified for an activity will help you to make appropriate judgements about children's capabilities and to record them systematically.

To collect information:

- talk to children about their activities and listen to their responses;

- listen to children talking to each other;

- observe children's work such as early writing, drawings, paintings and 3D models. (Keeping photocopies or photographs is sometimes useful.)

Sometimes you may wish to set up one-off activities for the purposes of monitoring development. Some groups, for example, ask children to make a drawing of themselves at the beginning of each term to record their progressing skills in both co-ordination and observation. Do not attempt to make records following every activity!

- **Reflective observations:** It is useful to spend regular time reflecting on the progress of a few children (about four each week). Aim to make some brief comments about each child every half term.

INFORMING YOUR PLANNING

Collecting evidence about children's progress is time consuming and it is important that it is useful. When you are planning, use the information you have collected to help you to decide what learning opportunities you need to provide next for children. For example, a child who has poor pencil or brush control will benefit from more play with dough or construction toys to build the strength of hand muscles.

Example of recording chart

Name: Edmund Field		D.O.B. 26.1.97		Date of entry: 13.9.00	
Term	**Personal, Social and Emotional Development**	**Communication Language and Literacy**	**Mathematical Development**	**Knowledge and Understanding of the World**	**Physical Development**	**Creative Development**
ONE	Starting to collaborate with peers. Prefers adult company. 20.9.00 EMH	Enjoying listening to stories. Titch a particular favourite. 20.11.00 EMH	Is able to say numbers to ten and to count accurately five objects. Recognises halves and quarters 5.11.00 SJS	Very keen on flowers. Brought in examples of pressed flowers from home. 16.10.00 EC	Can hop. Finds using and ball difficult. 16.10.00 AC	Enjoyed gluing and cutting. Made a wonderful model caravan. 20.10.00 LSS
TWO						
THREE						

SKILLS OVERVIEW OF SIX WEEK PLAN

Week	Topic focus	Personal, Social and Emotional Development	Communication Language and Literacy	Mathematical Development	Knowledge and Understanding of the World	Physical Development	Creative Development
1	Detecting Summer	Sharing Playing collaboratively Being sensitive to others	Talking Writing Describing	Estimating Measuring Recognising number	Investigating Recording	Fine motor skills Moving with control	Making sounds Listening Painting
2	Summer fruits	Being aware of health and safety	Role play Describing	Sorting Exploring pattern Counting	Comparing Using materials	Moving with control Moving imaginatively	Using different media Printing
3	Summer flowers	Discussing feelings Appreciation of the environment	Comparing Rhyming Recognising letters	Comparing Sorting Counting Repeating patterns	Investigating Observing	Aiming Throwing Playing collaboratively	Finger painting Sewing Modelling
4	Sunny week	Awareness of safety Care of others	Sequencing Telling stories	Repeating patterns Matching shape Awareness of time	Observing Investigating Using materials	Fine motor skills Moving with imagination and awareness of space	Gluing Using materials
5	Summer holidays	Sharing Discussing feelings and behaviour	Role play Describing Early writing	Measuring time Recognising numbers	Describing Comparing	Using large apparatus Moving with awareness of space	Role play Modelling
6	Sports Day	Discussing feelings	Writing names Early writing Discussing	Ordinal numbers Comparing	Naming body parts Observing changes	Gross and fine motor skills Moving with imagination	Miming Blow painting

HOME LINKS

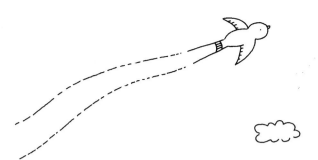

The theme of Summer lends itself to useful links with children's homes and families. Through working together children and adults gain respect for each other and build comfortable and confident relationships.

ESTABLISHING PARTNERSHIPS

- Keep parents informed about the topic of Summer, and the themes for each week. By understanding the work of the group, parents will enjoy the involvement of contributing ideas, time and resources.

- Request parental permission before taking children out of the group on a Summer walk. Describe your route and the purposes of the activity. Additional parental help will be necessary for this activity to be carried out safely.

- Photocopy the parent's page for each child to take home.

- Invite friends, childminders and families to share the sports day.

VISITING ENTHUSIASTS

- Invite adults from other cultures to show children how some of the less familiar fruits and vegetables are used in traditional recipes.

- Sporting enthusiasts may be willing to come into the group to talk about their interests.

RESOURCE REQUESTS

- Encourage contributions of Summer finds from family walks.

- Ask to borrow summer coloured fabrics or seasonal pictures which could be used for displays.

PREPARING FOR SPORTS DAY

- Request adult help in making any small prizes, such as ribbon rosettes which are to be awarded at the sports day event.